This coloring book b

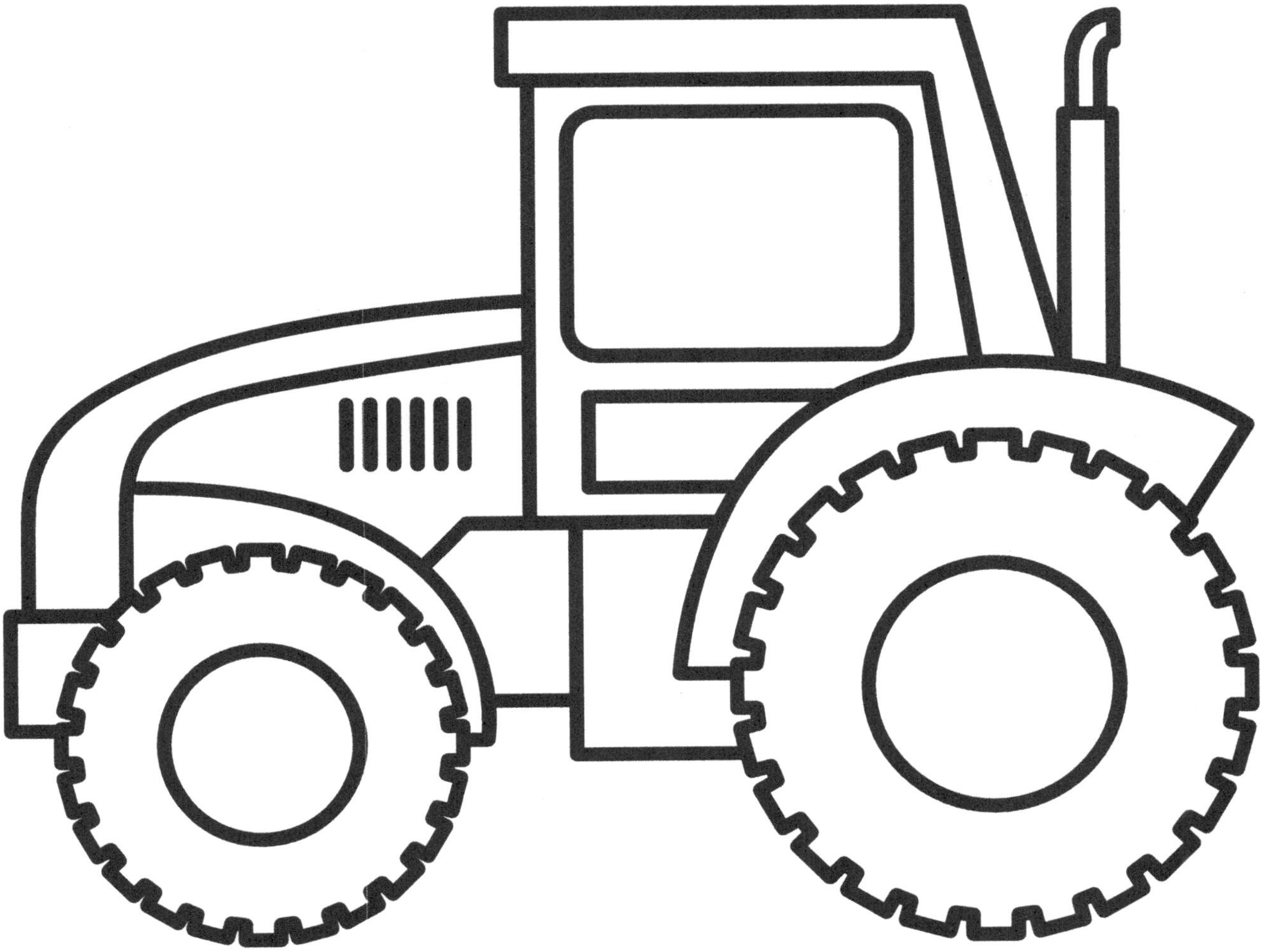

First Edition: 2019

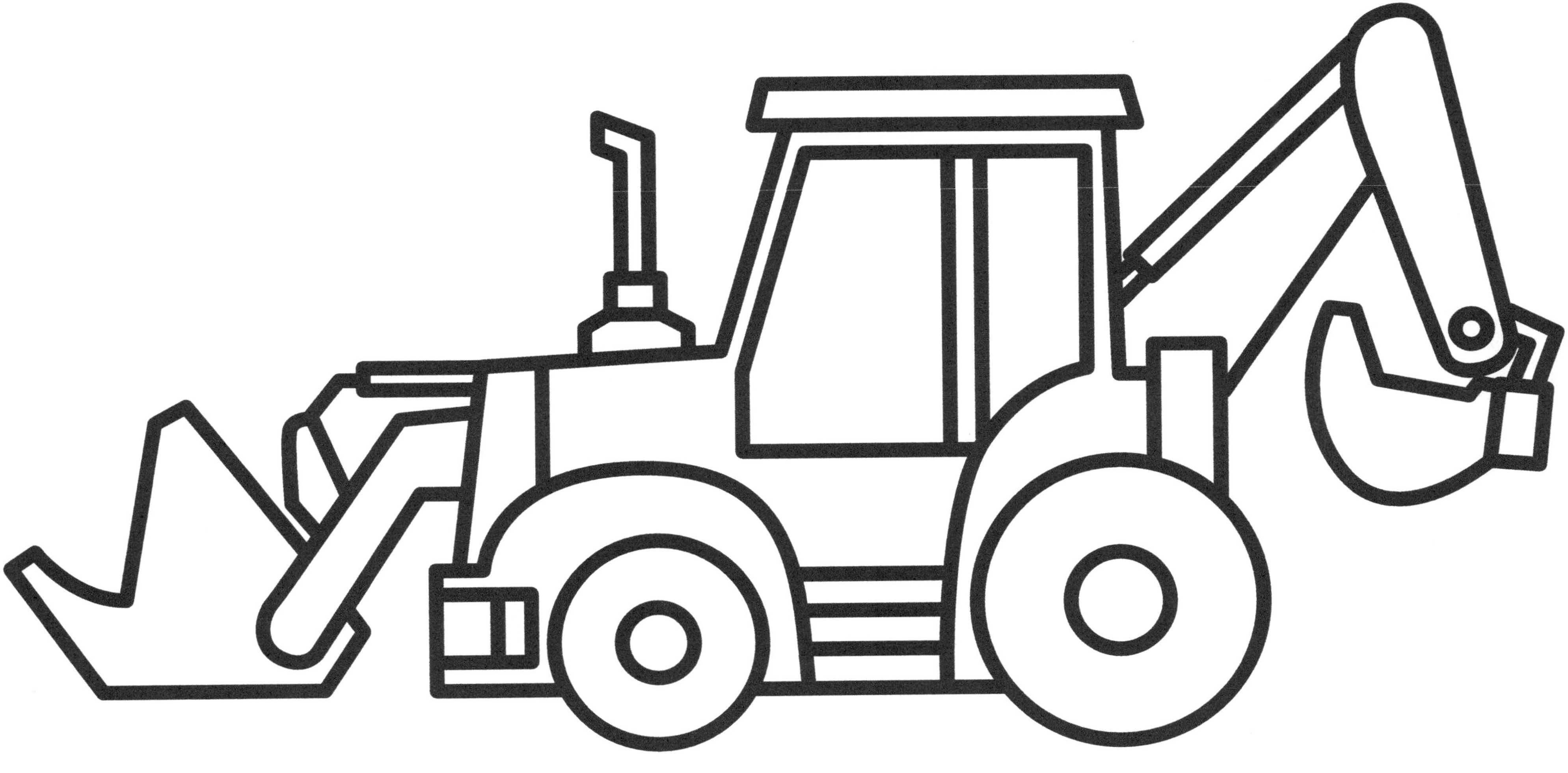

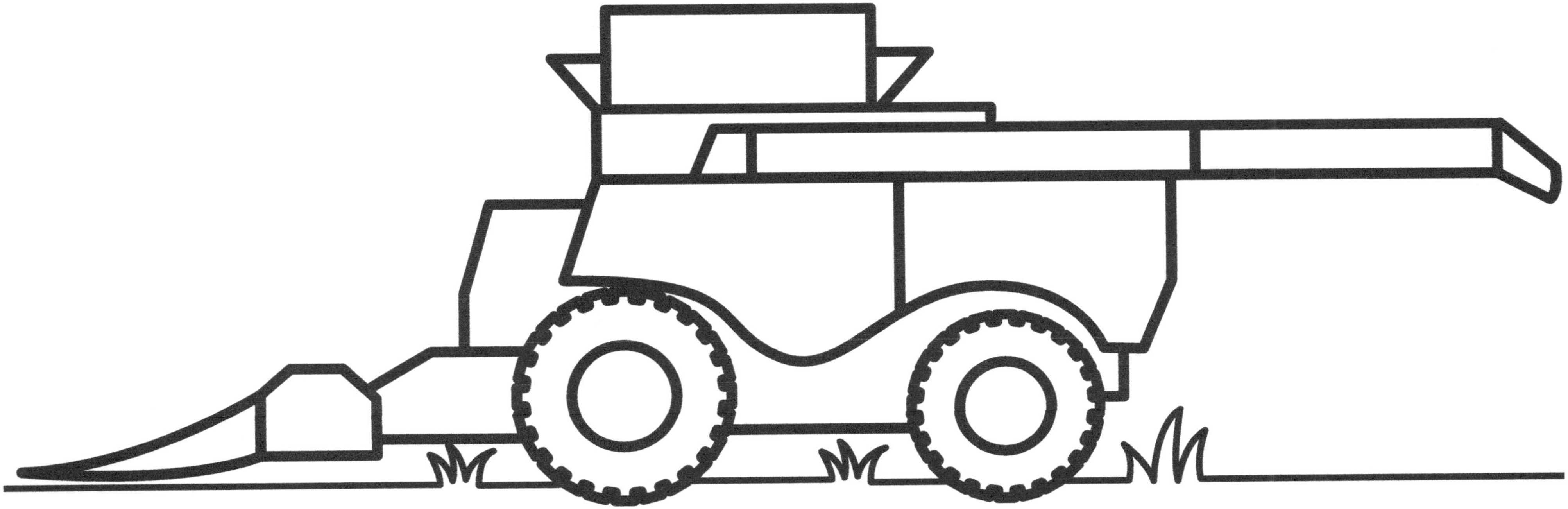

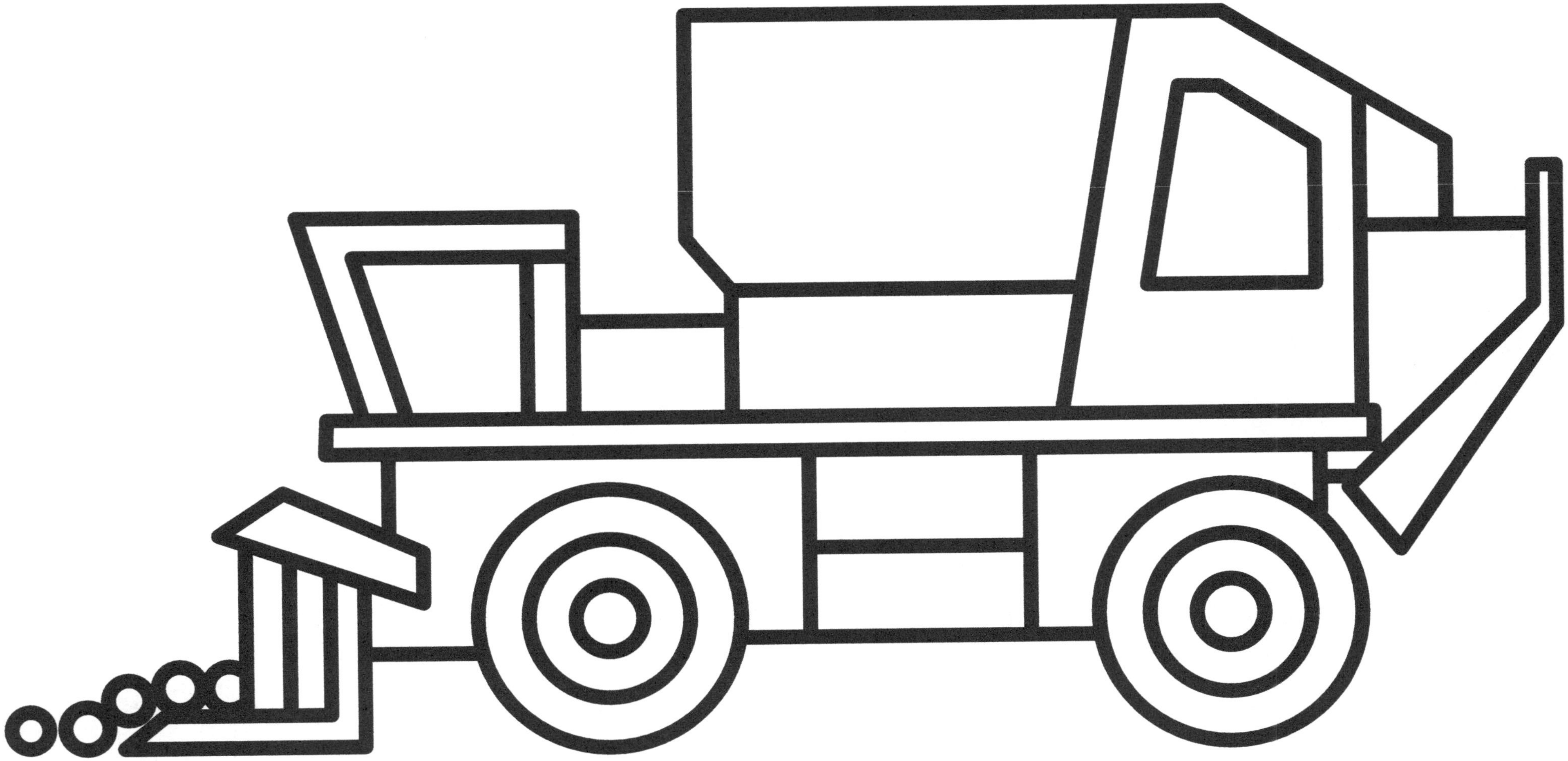

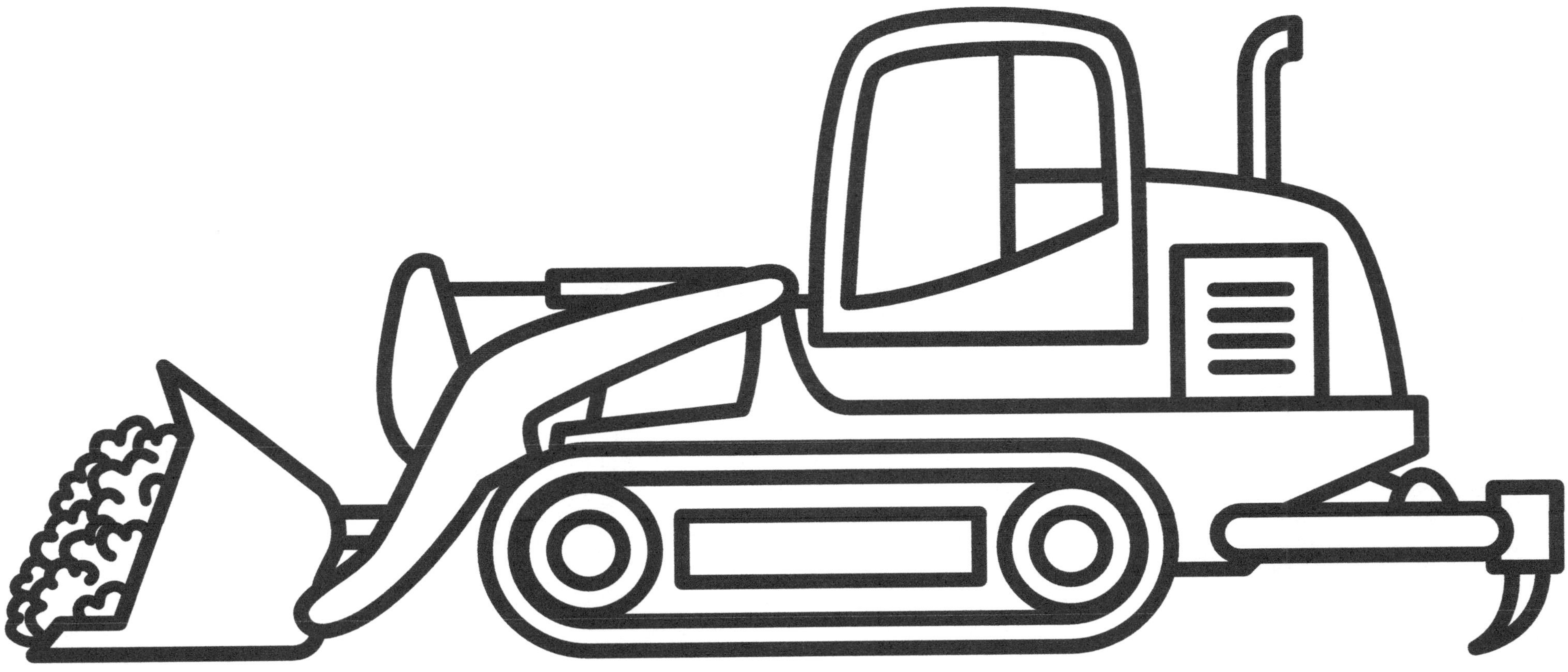

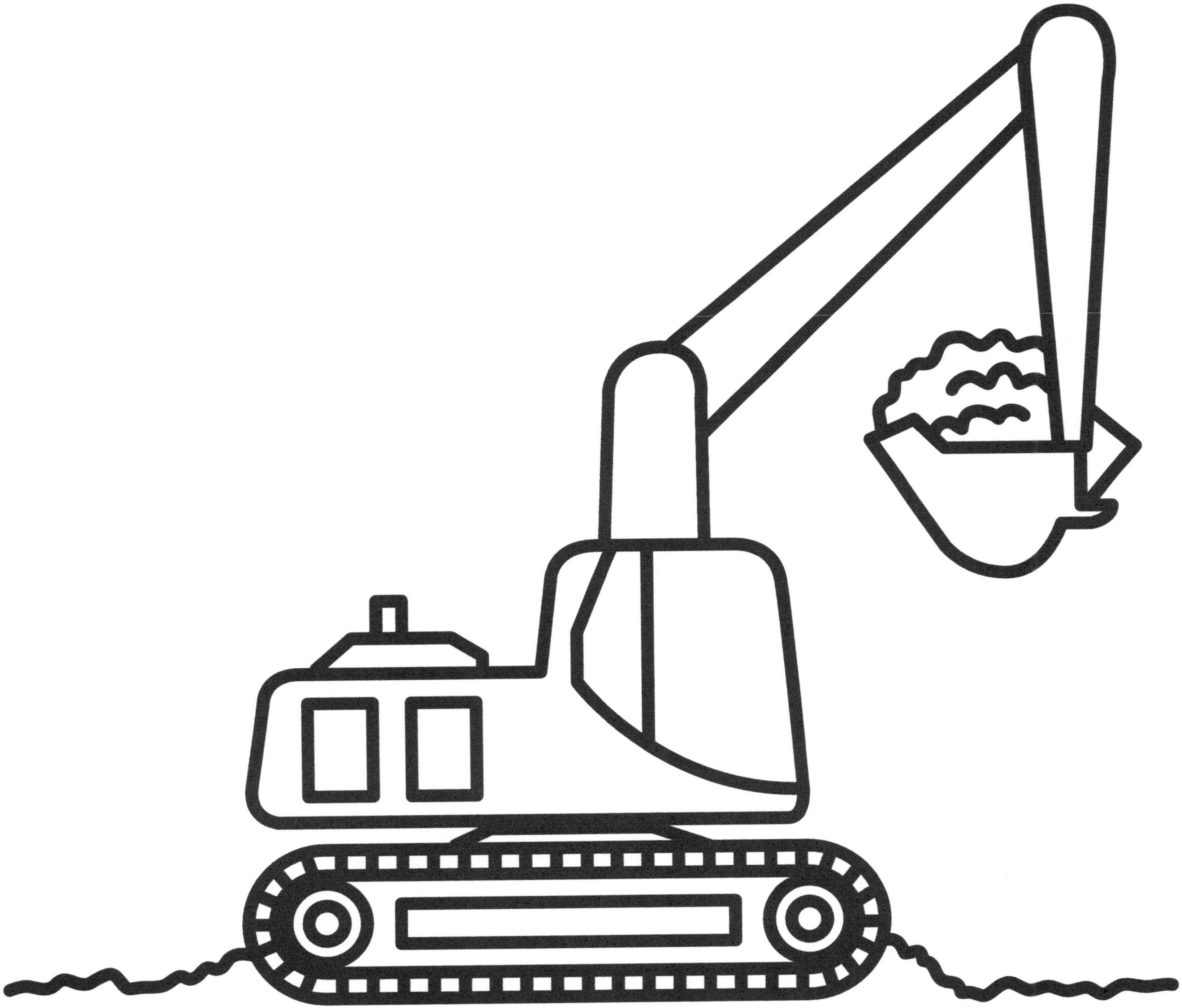

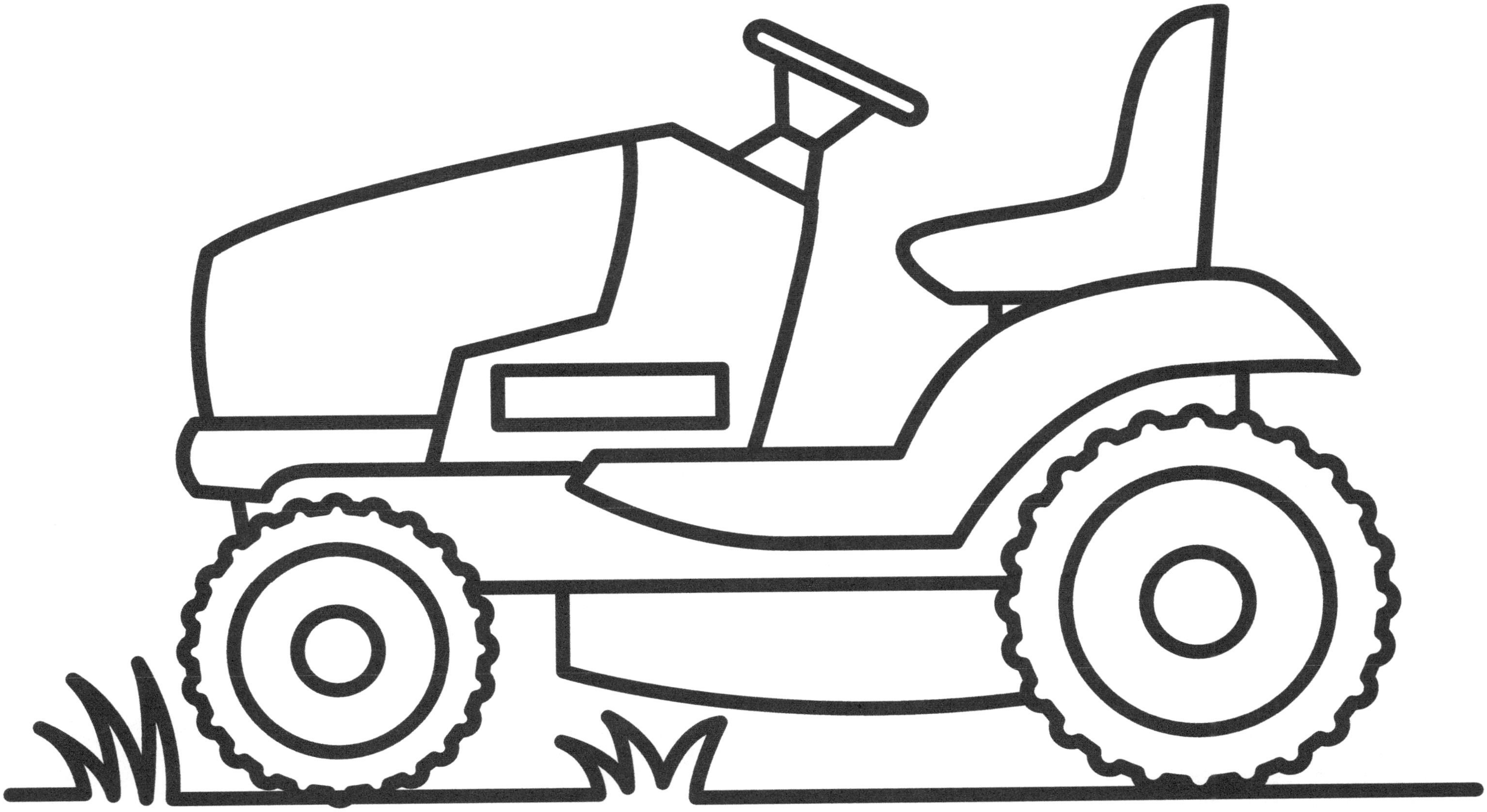

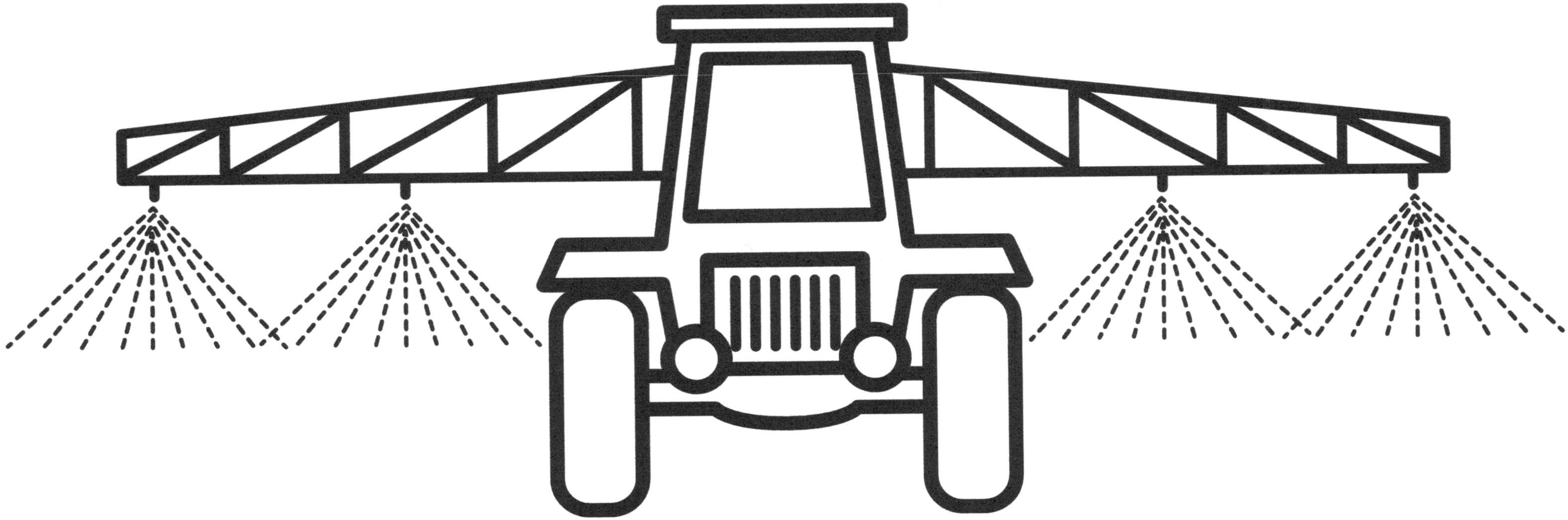

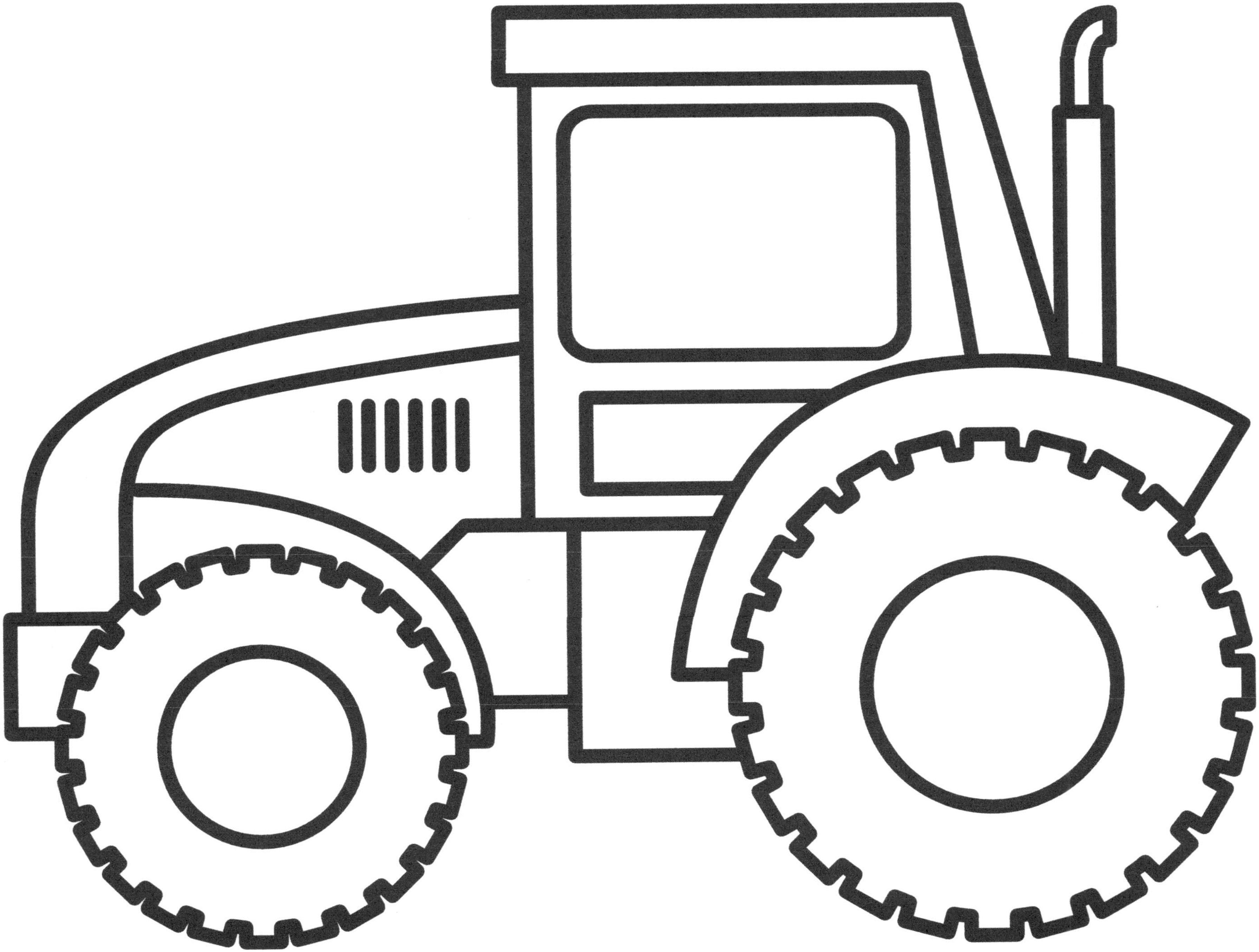

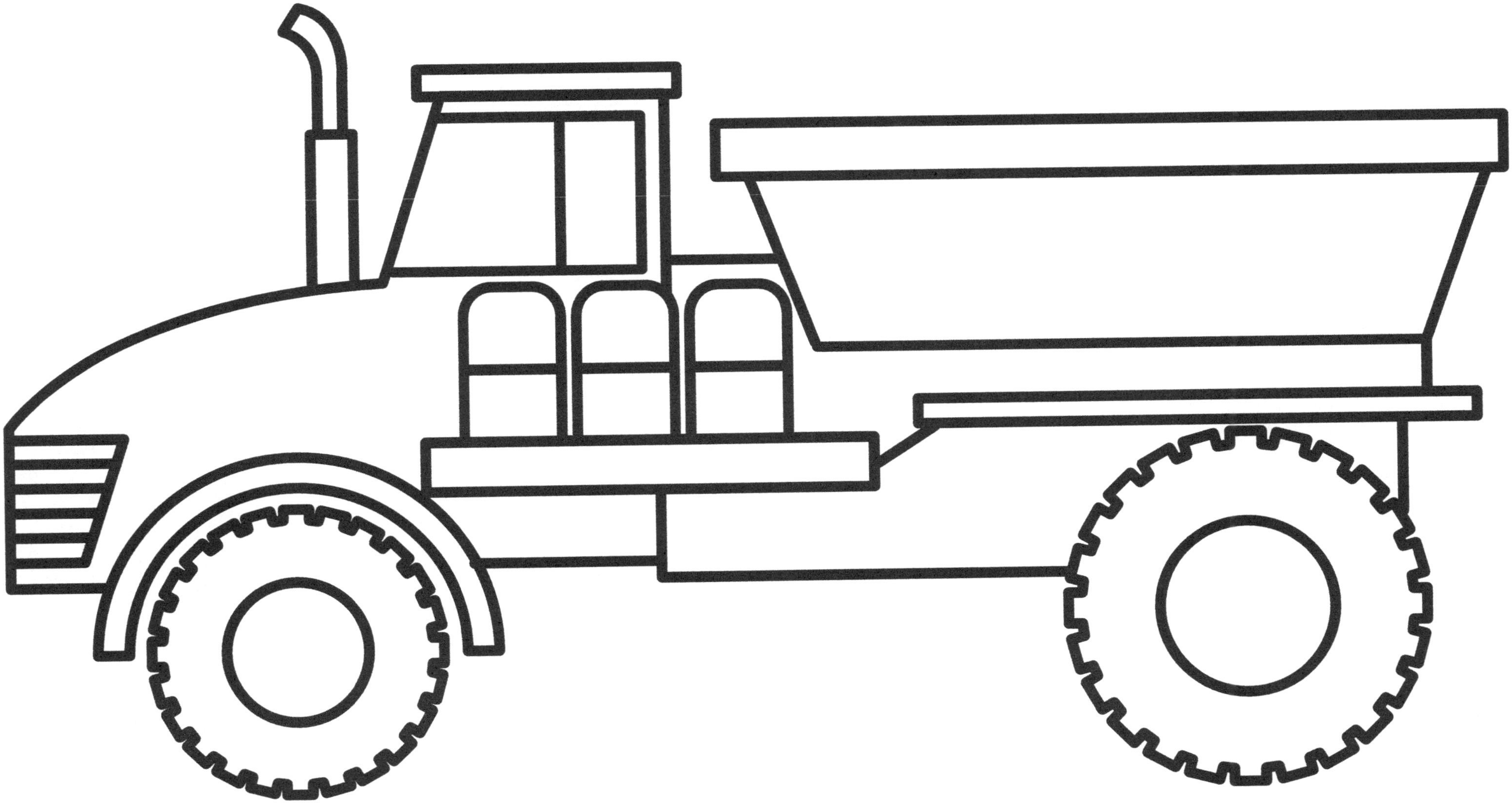

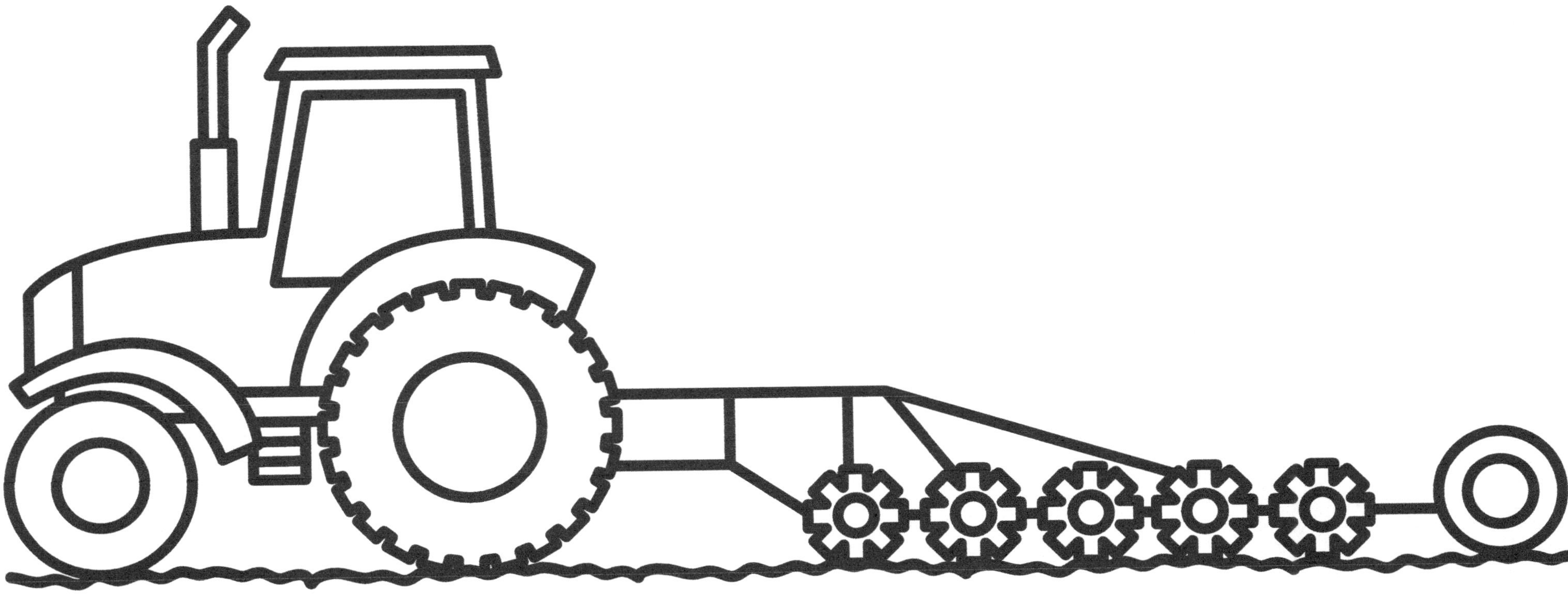

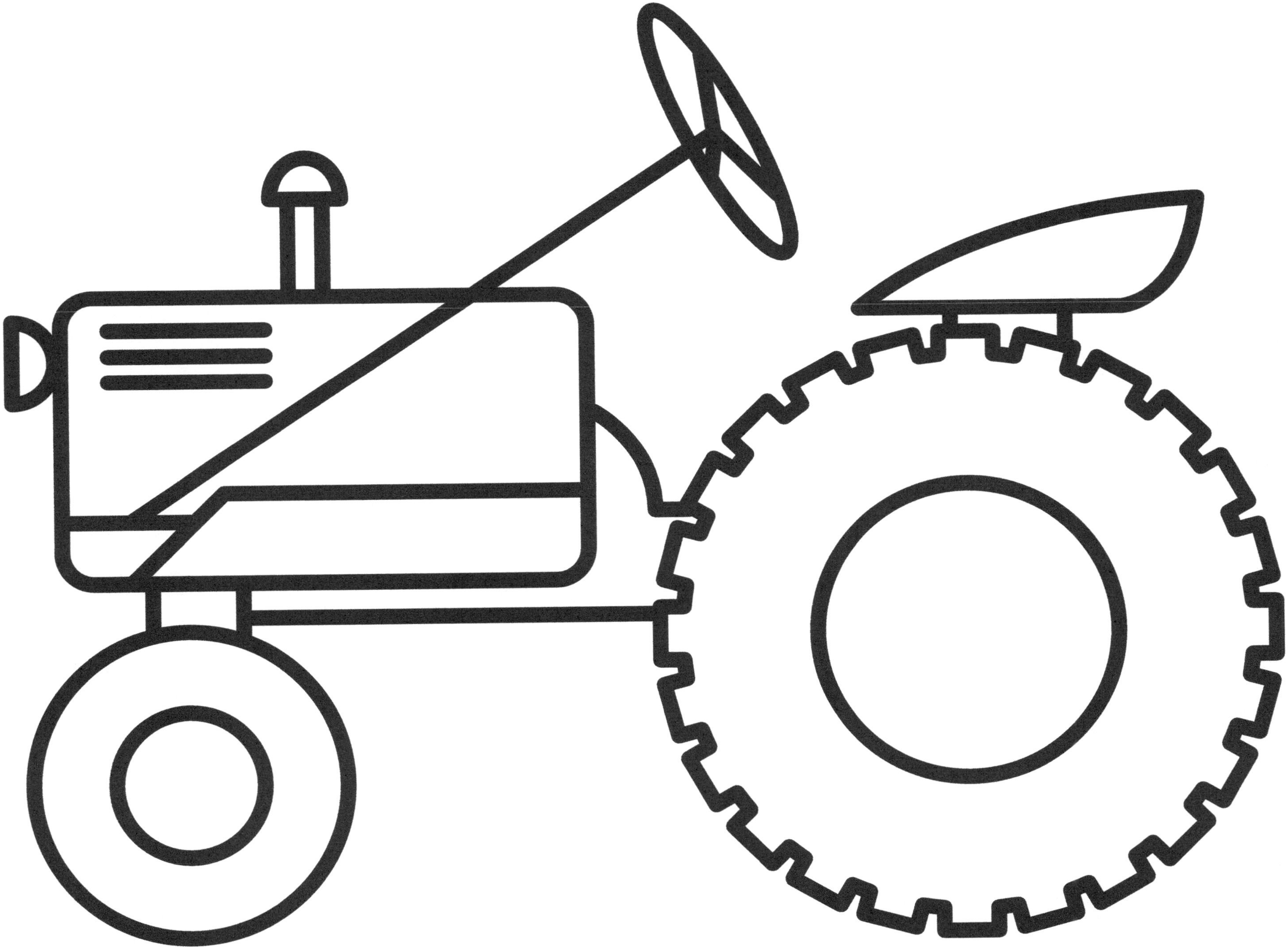

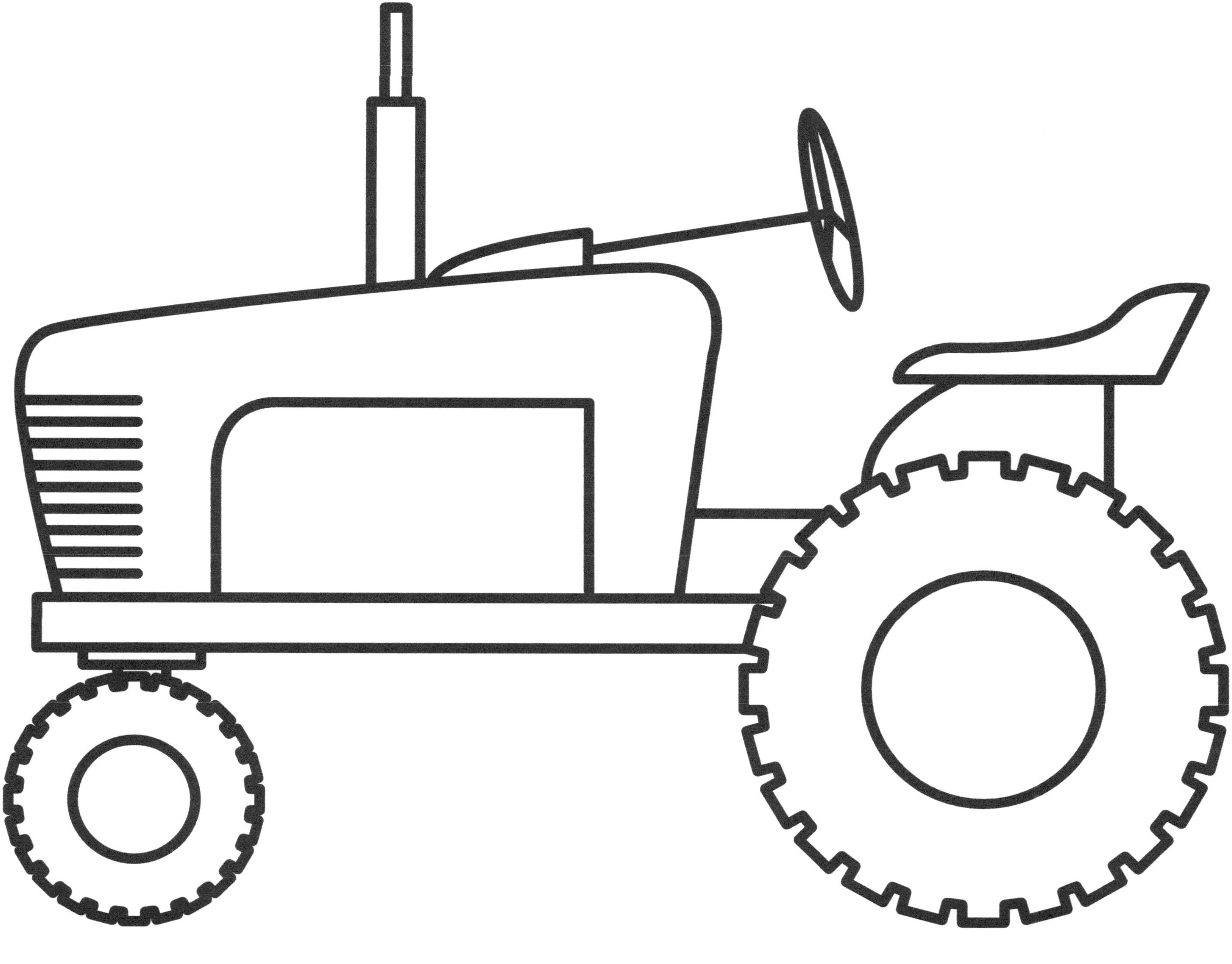

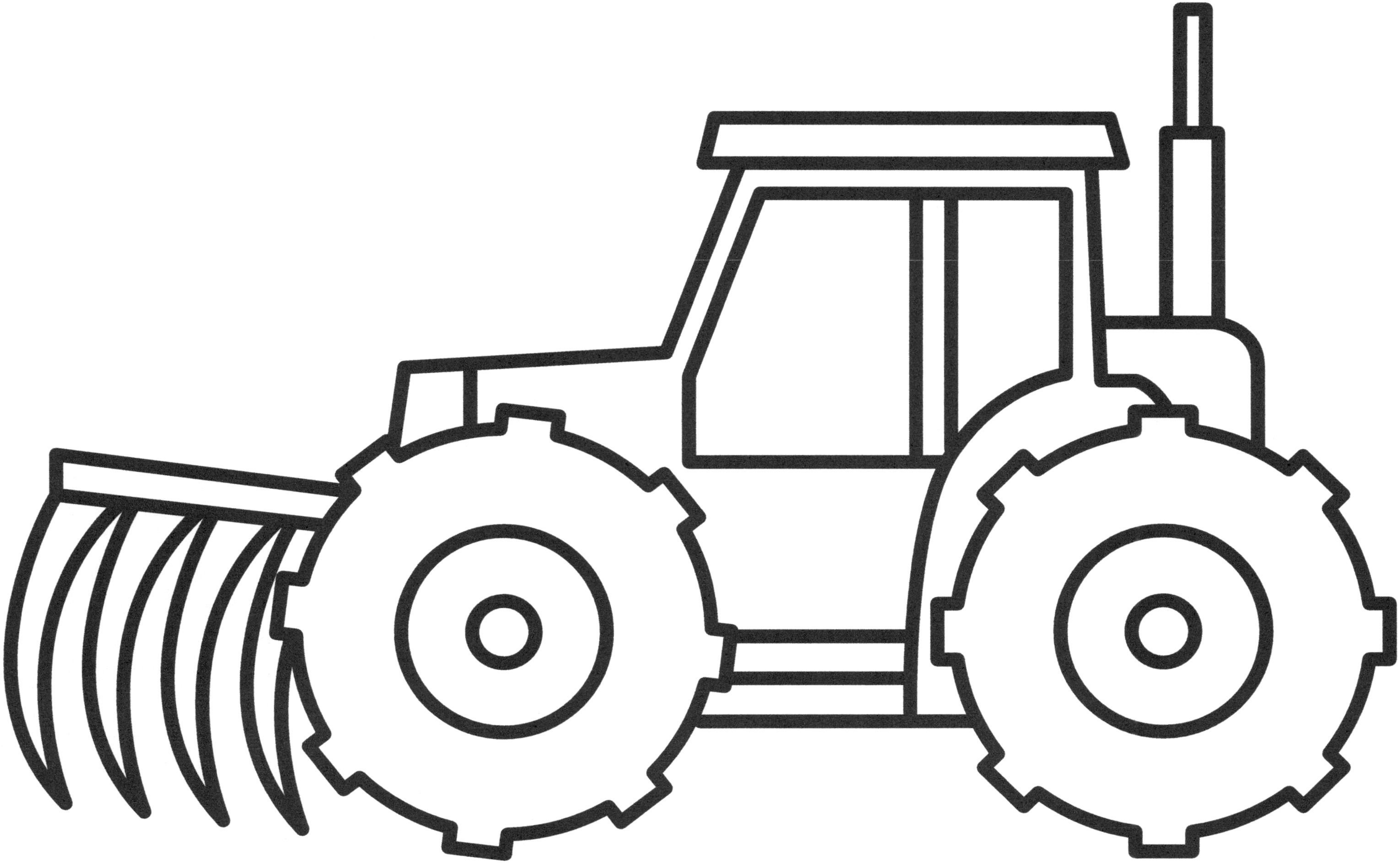

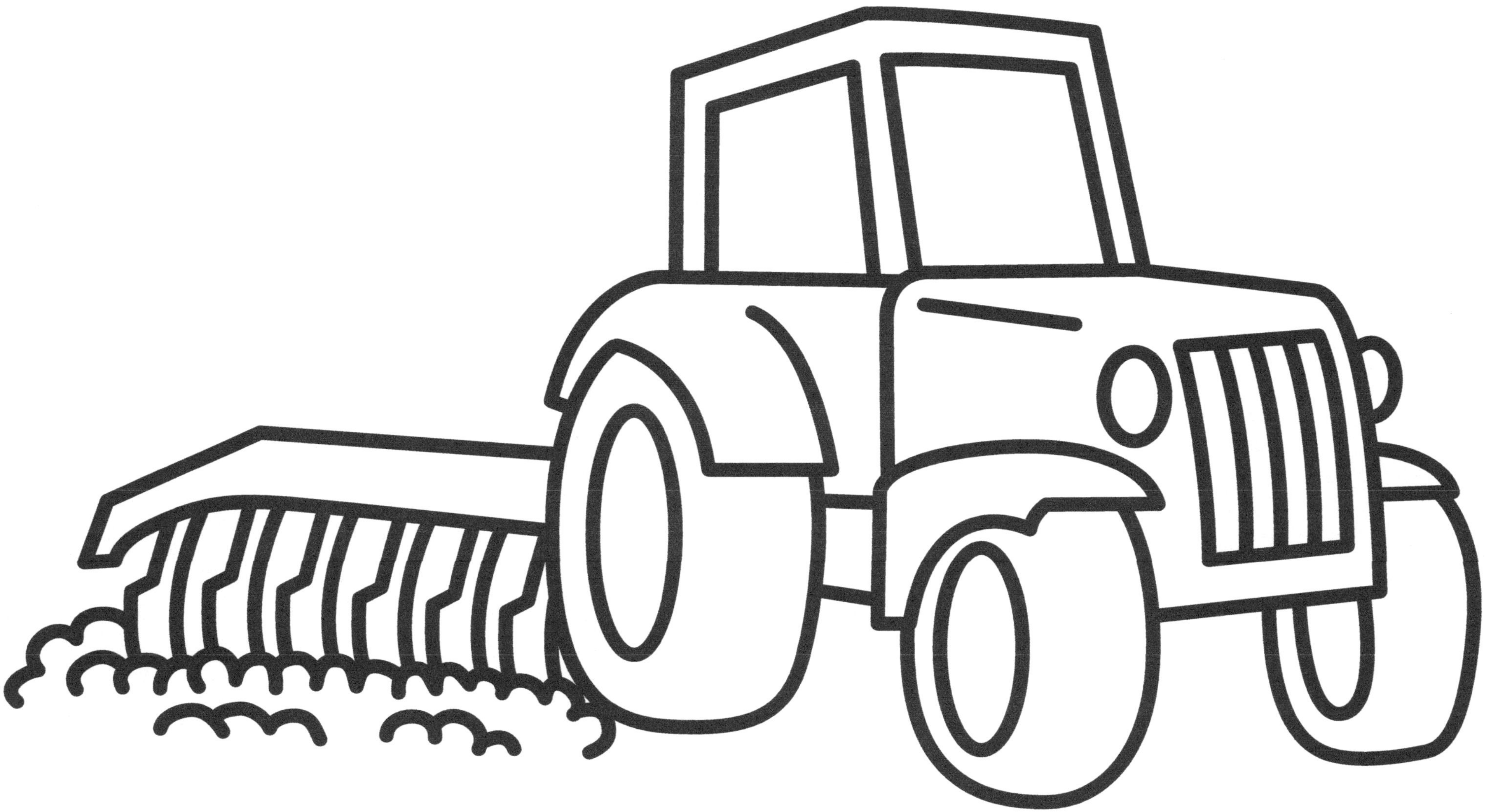

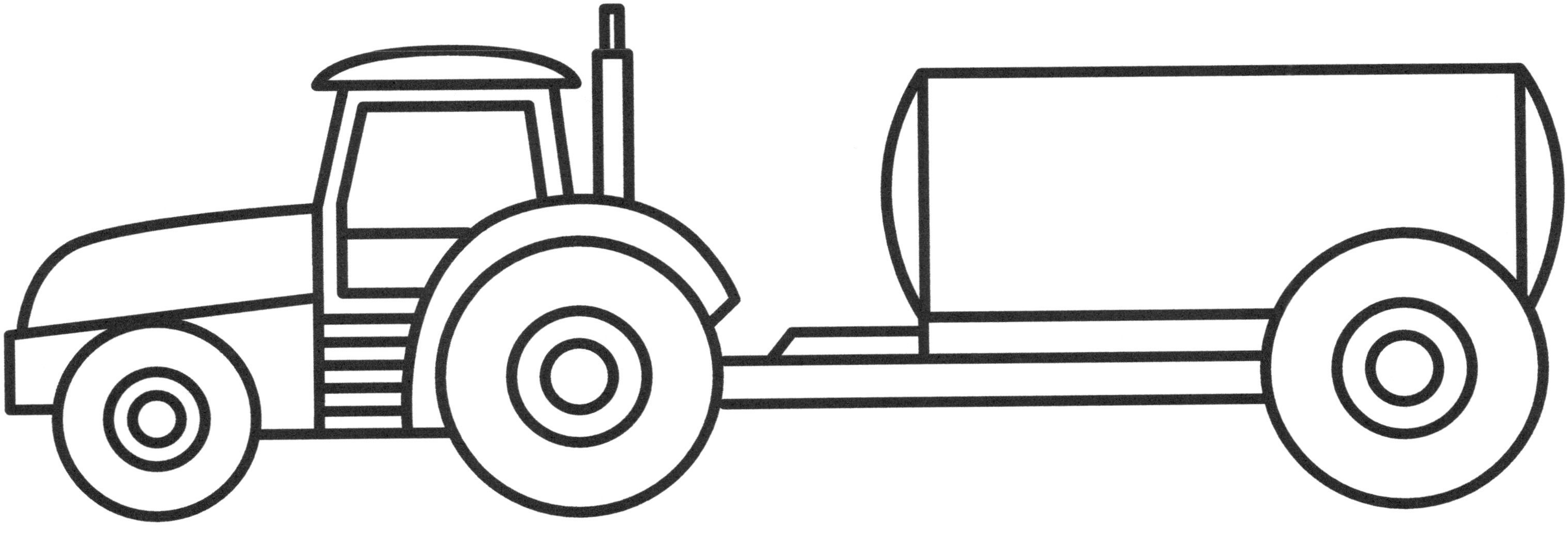

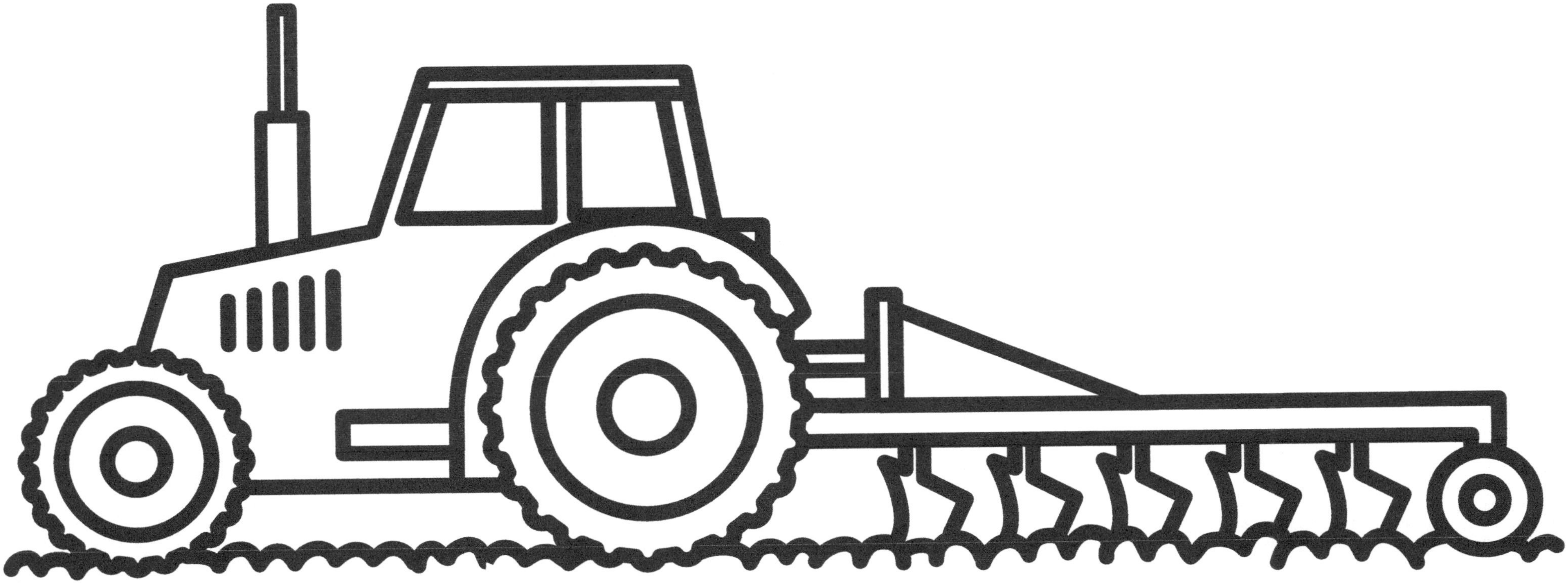

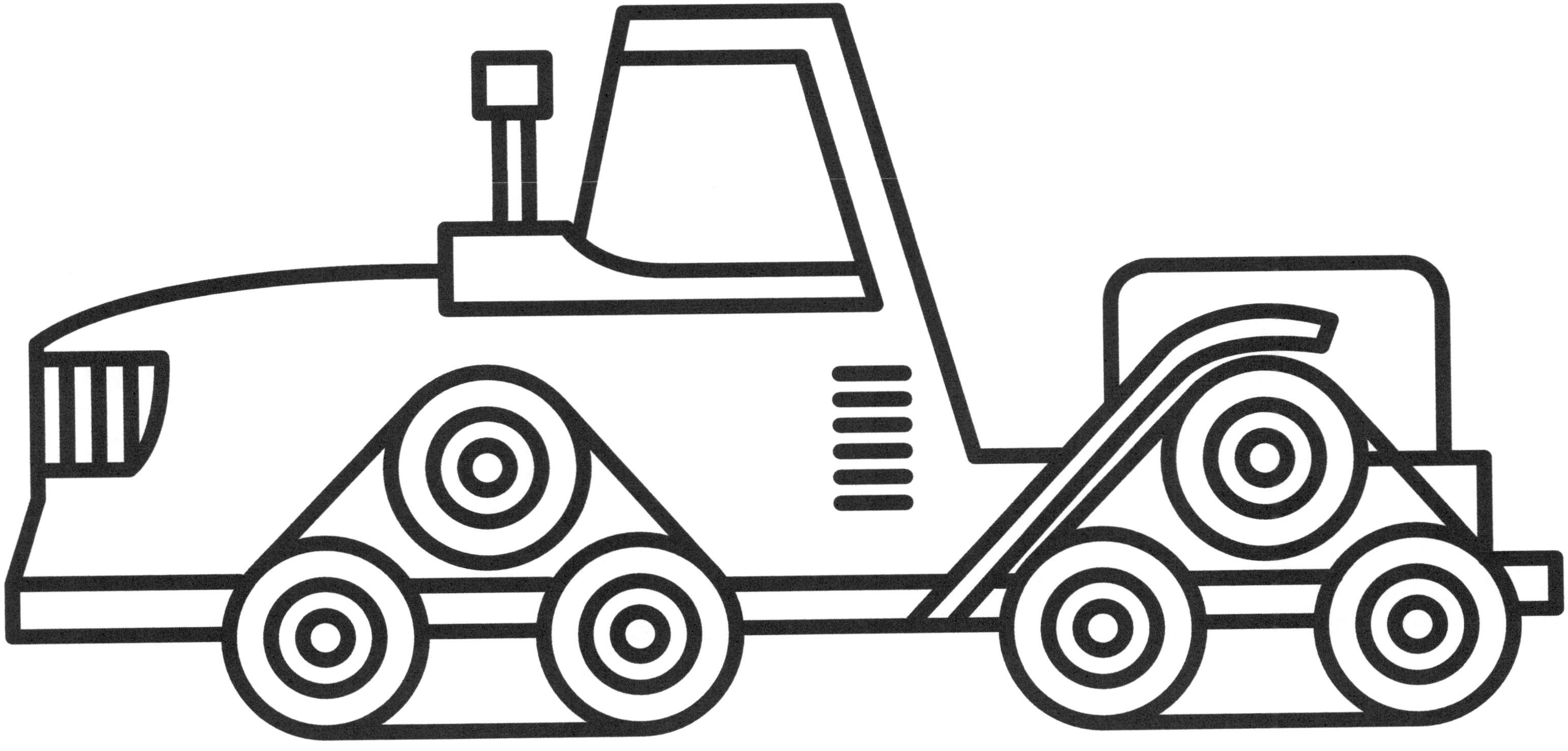

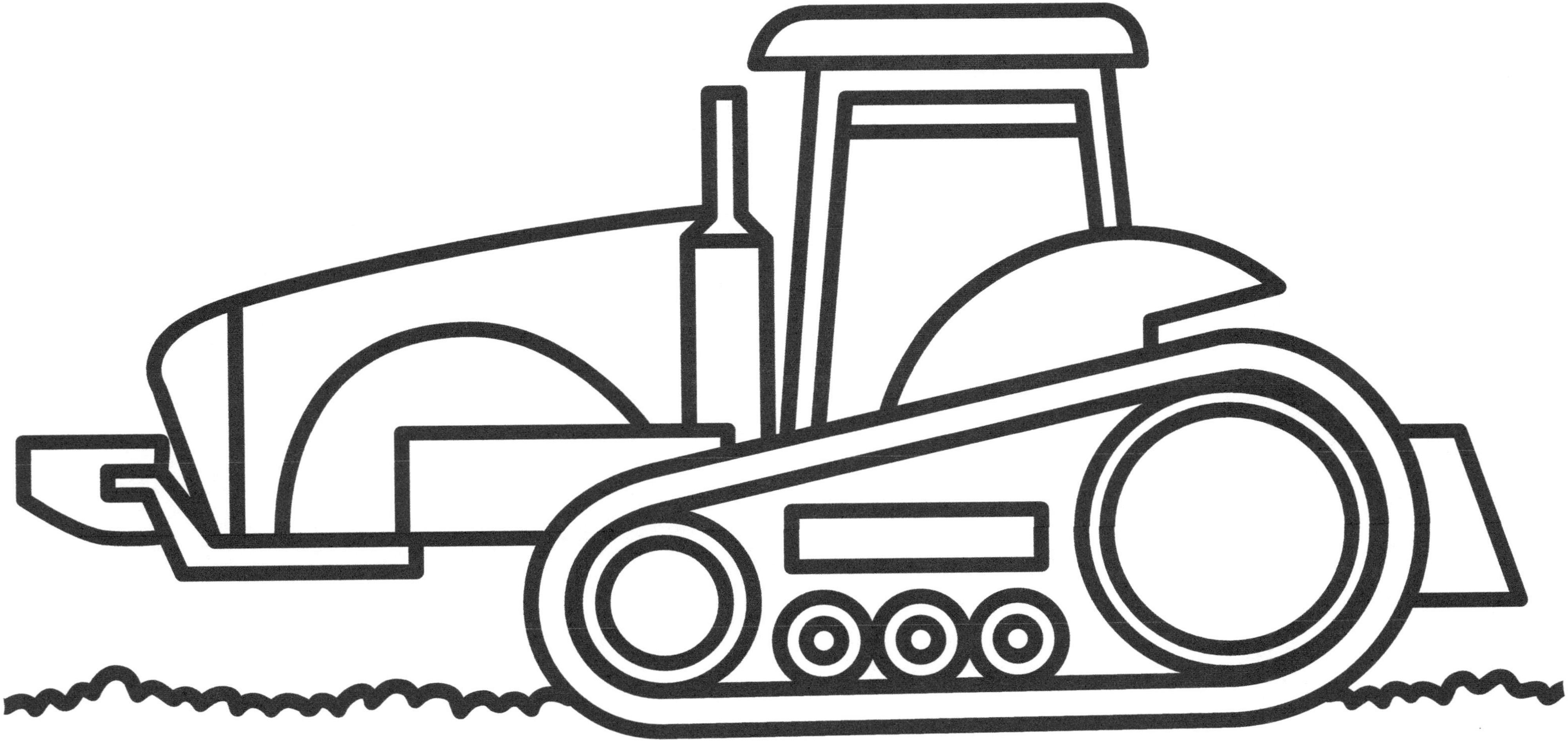

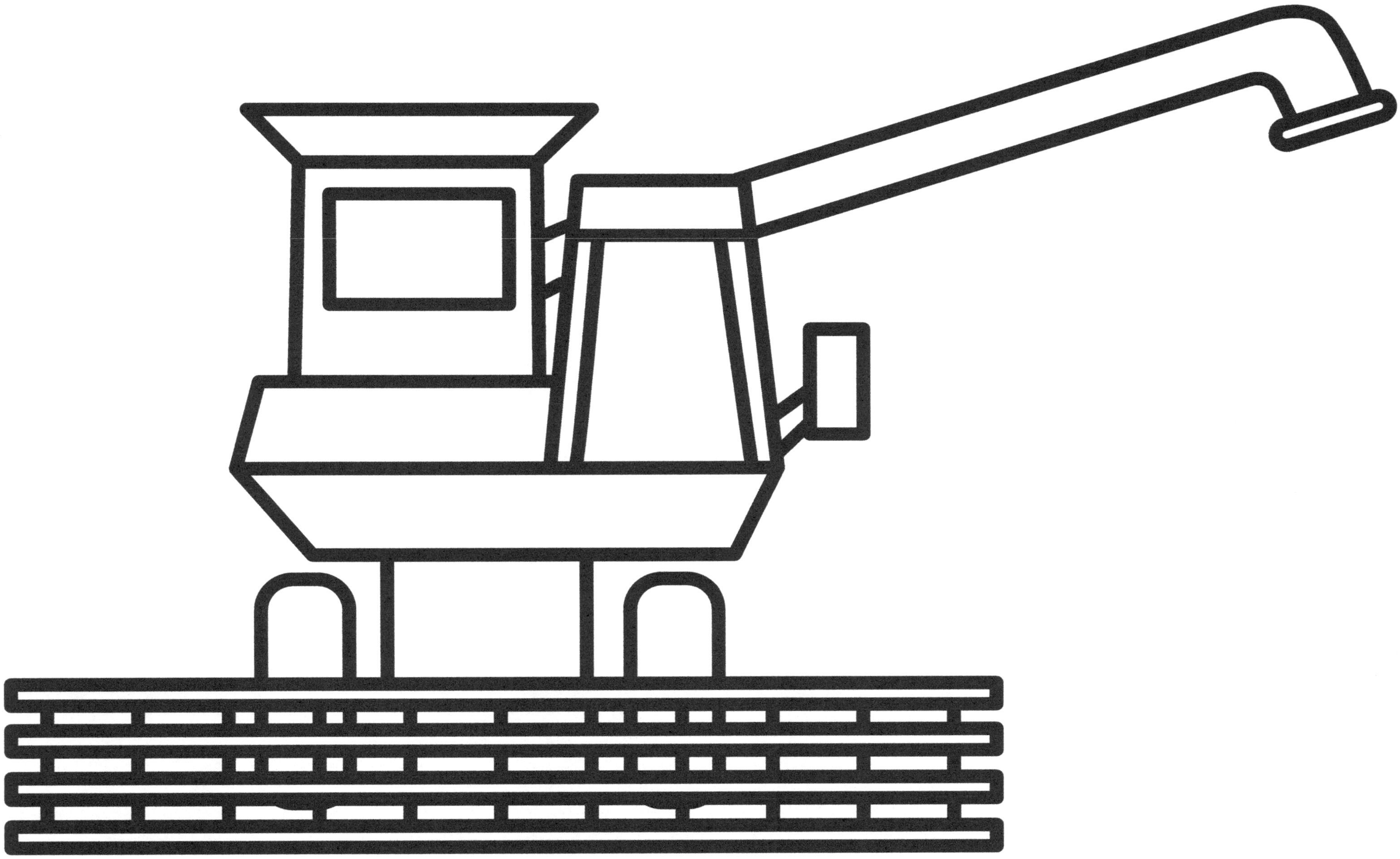

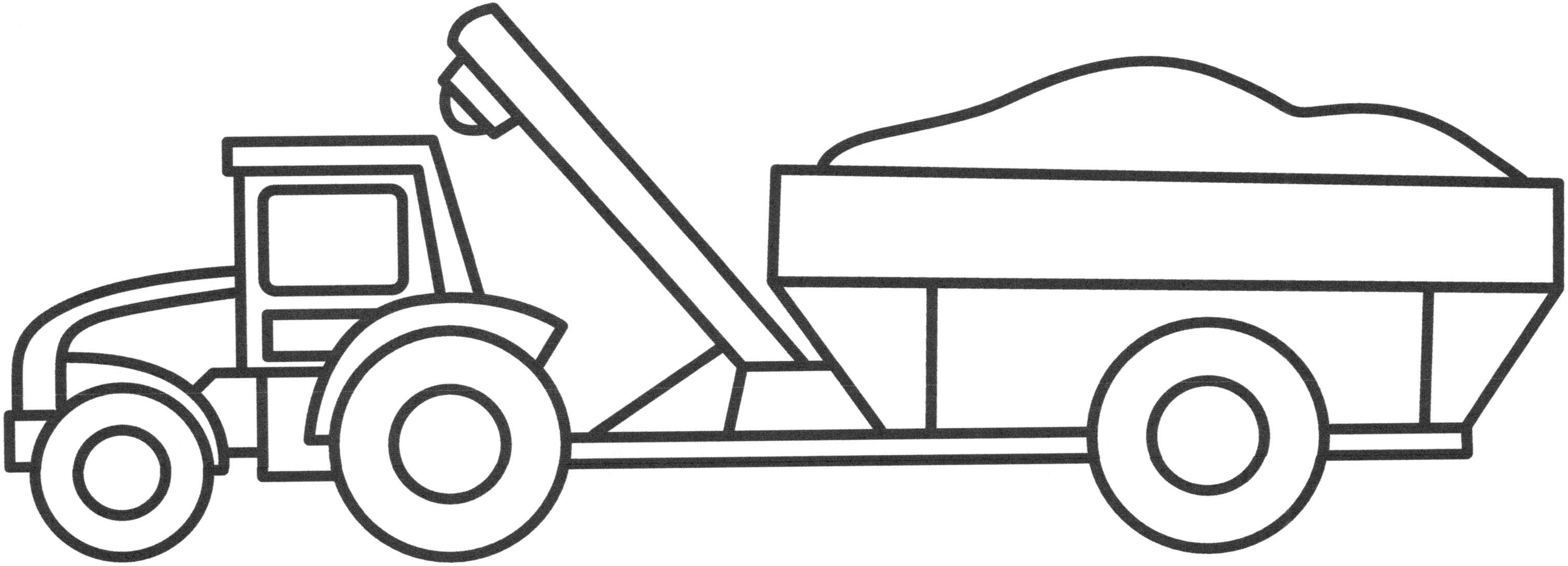

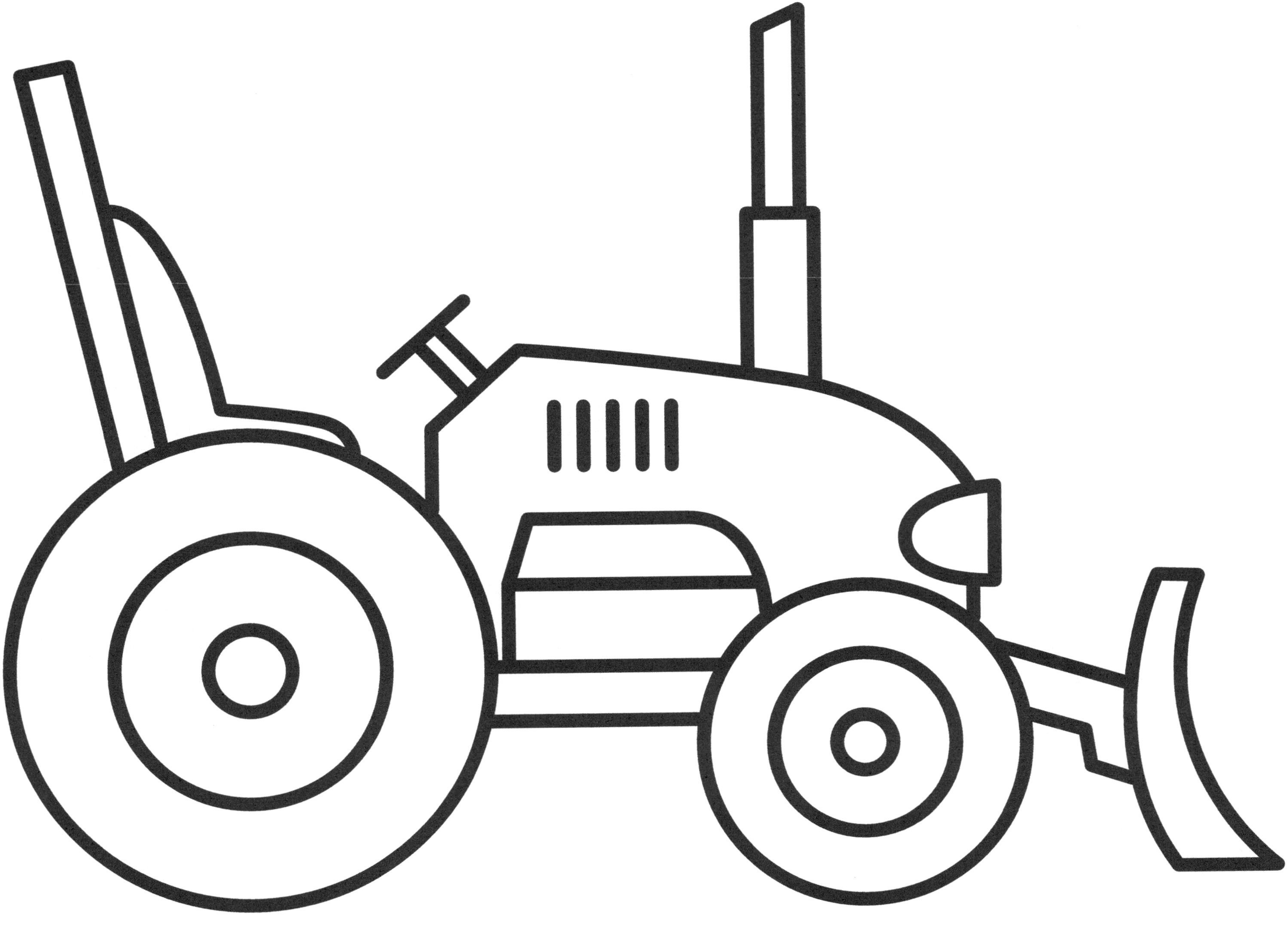

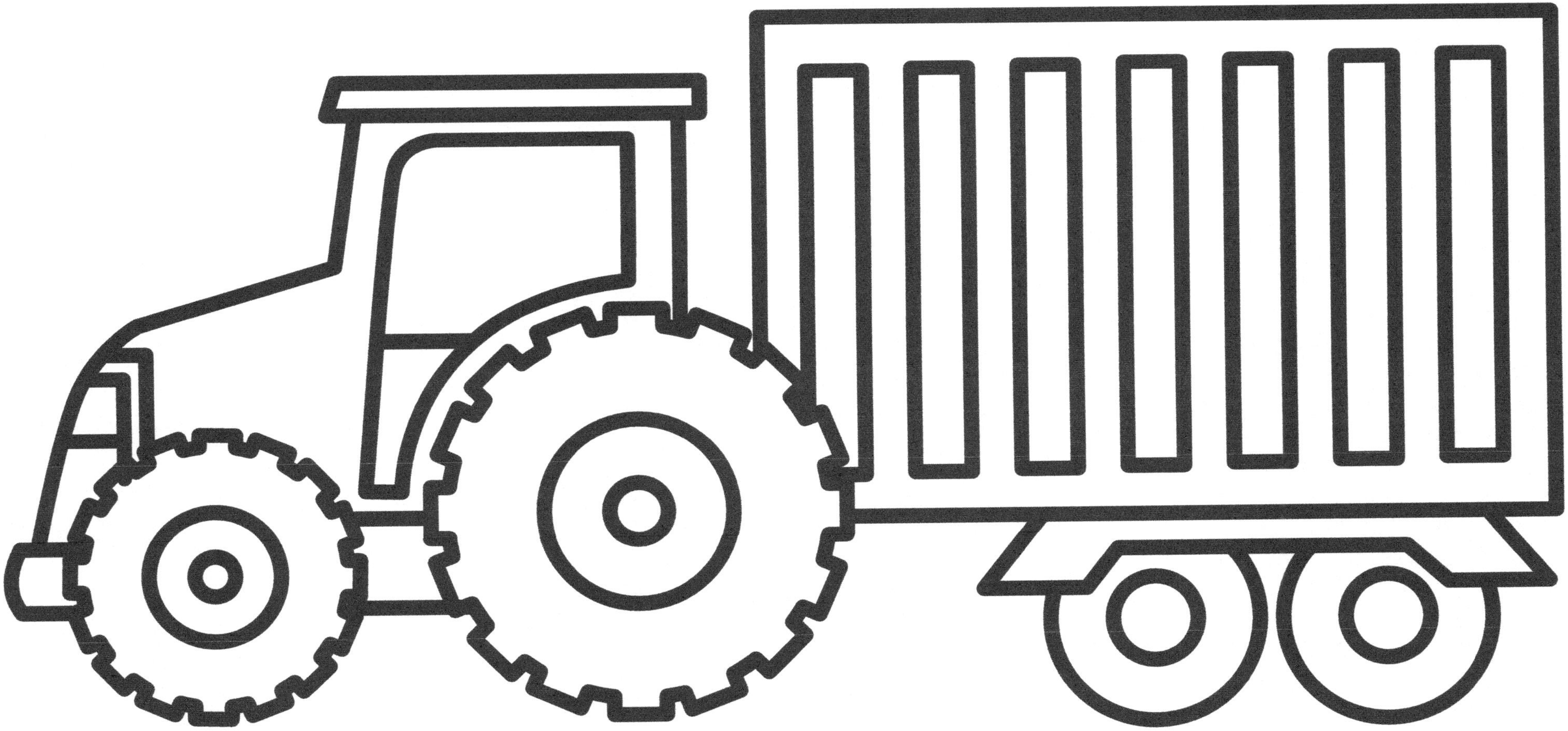

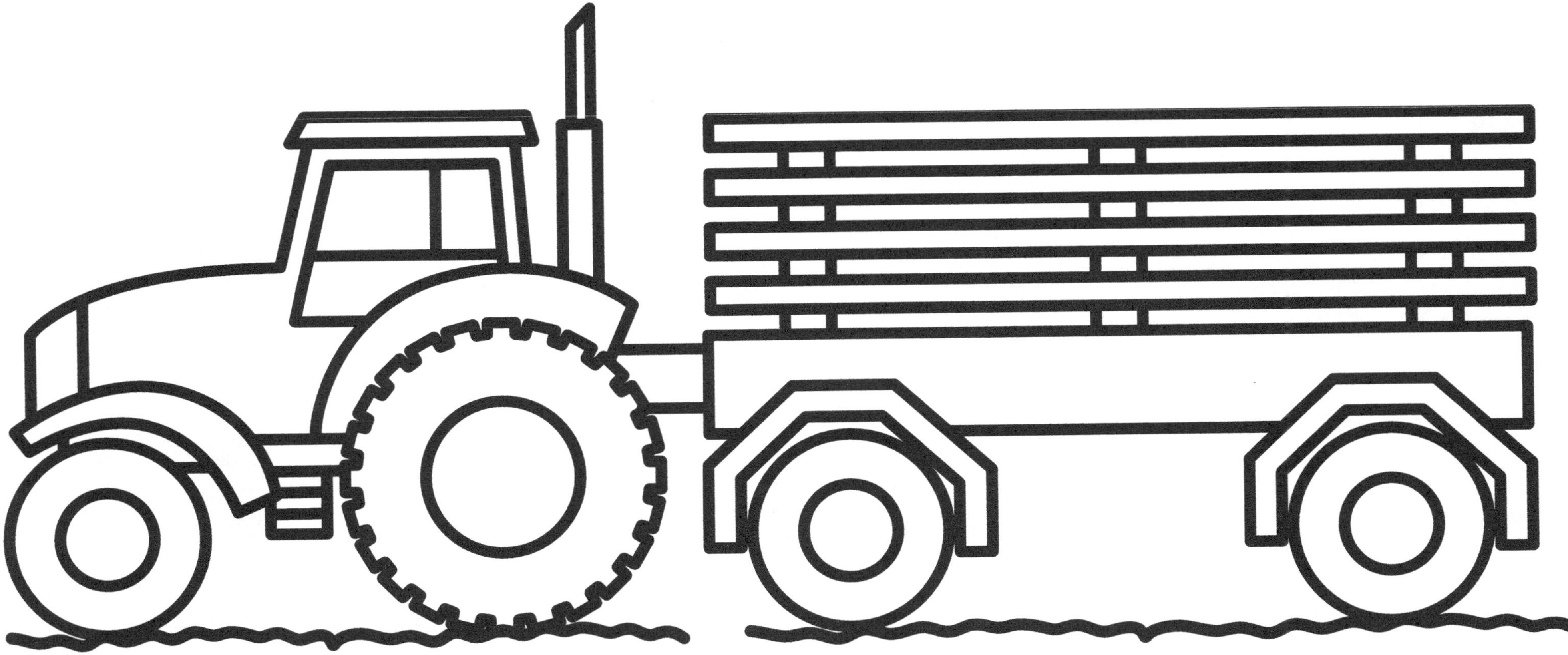

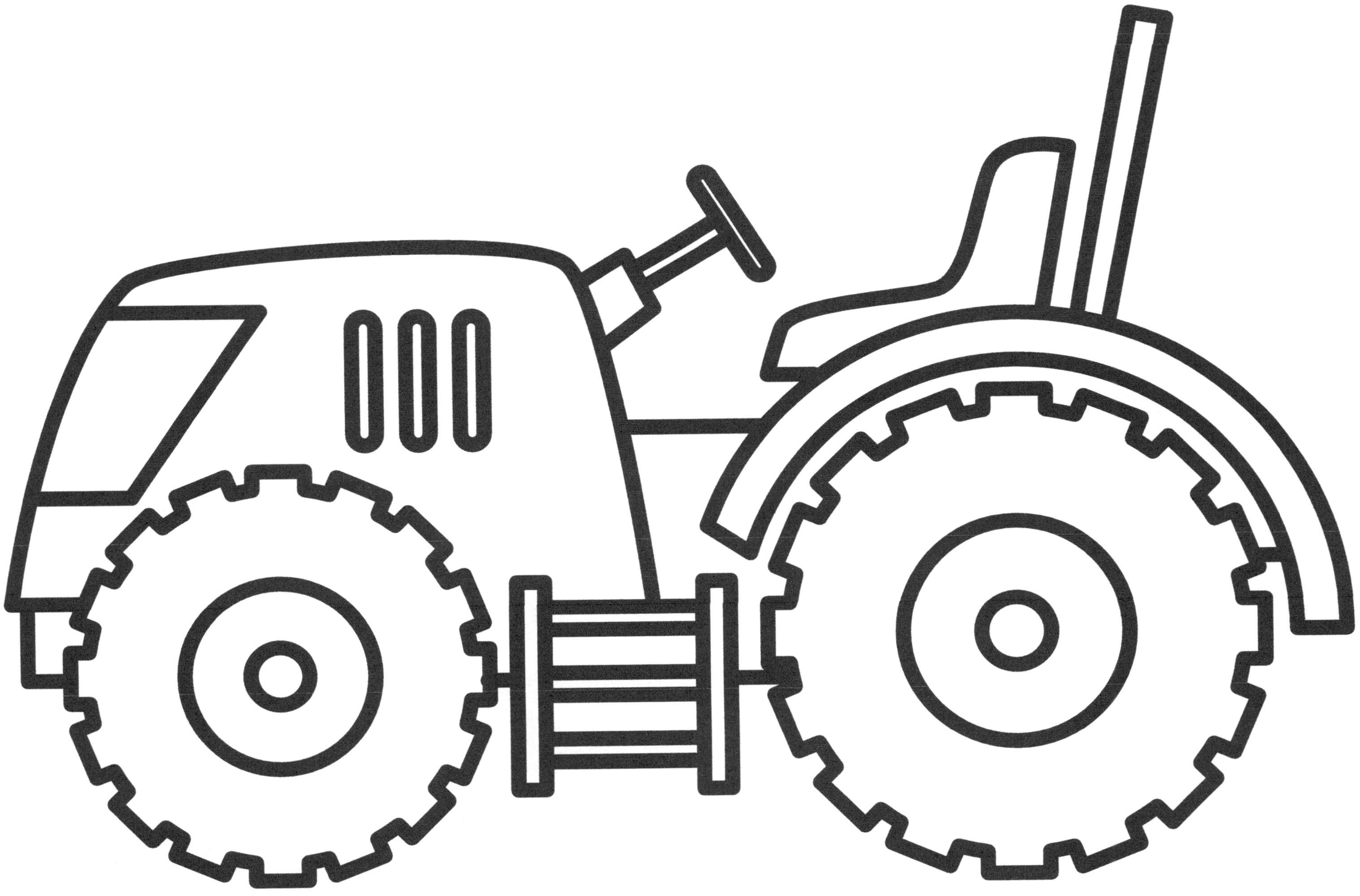

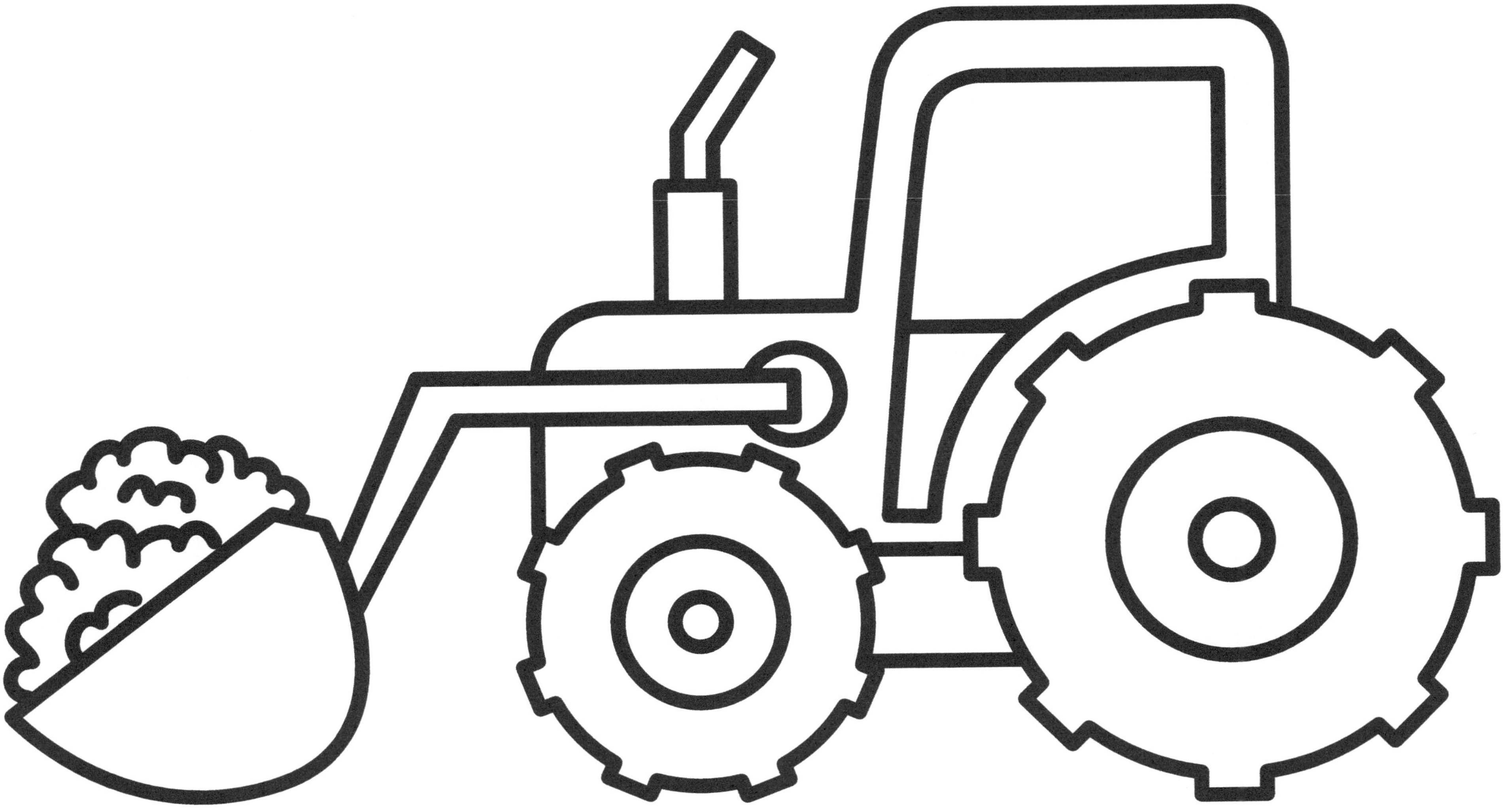

Made in the USA
Coppell, TX
19 November 2023

24485957R00031